Adventures of the Letter I

Other books by Louis Simpson

LOUIS SIMPSON

Adventures of the Letter I

1817

HARPER & ROW, PUBLISHERS

New York
Evanston
San Francisco
London

Acknowledgments are due to editors of the following magazines, in which some of the poems first appeared: *The American Scholar, Chelsea, The Critical Quarterly, Field, Fire Exit, Harper's Magazine, kayak, The Listener, London Magazine, The Nation, New Mexico Quarterly, The New Statesman, The Poetry Review, The Quarterly Review, The Review, The Sixties, Stony Brook, Sumac.*

"Life, the Interesting Character," "Vandergast and the Girl," "The Country House," and "Adam Yankev" originally appeared in *The New Yorker.*

"Simplicity," "Cynthia," and "Sensibility" originally appeared in *The Southern Review.*

"Love and Poetry" reprinted by permission of The Washington Post Company.

"Sacred Objects" was written for Walt Whitman on the occasion of his sesquicentennial birthday celebration, May 31, 1969. It was read by Louis Simpson on this date at Walt Whitman's birthplace in Huntington, Long Island.

"American Dreams" first appeared in *A Poetry Reading vs the Vietnam War* published by American Writers vs the Vietnam War in 1966.

FIRST EDITION

STANDARD BOOK NUMBER: 06-013884-X

LIBRARY OF CONGRESS CATALOG CARD NUMBER: 74-138762

For Matthew, Anthony, and Anne

CONTENTS

V The Foggy Lane

I

Volhynia Province

When I was a child we lived in a house called Volyn, after Volhynia, the part of Russia where my mother was born. Volhynia was the greatest imaginable distance from the island on which we lived. It snowed a great deal in Volhynia; there were wolves, Cossacks, and gypsies.

Since then I have learned that the people of Volhynia were poor and afraid of many things. They died in epidemics, the 'Volhynia fever' for which the province is noted in medical dictionaries. Yet some of them were scholars and cigarette-smoking intellectuals.

I have come to think of the country around Lutsk, where my mother's people lived, as a muddy plain with a dismal climate. Yet recently I met a Polish drama-critic who remembered spending a fortnight on the river near Lutsk canoeing with a girl. She was dressed like a Viennese and carried a blue parasol.

DVONYA

In the town of Odessa
there is a garden
and Dvonya is there,
Dvonya whom I love
though I have never been in Odessa.

I love her black hair, and eyes
as green as a salad
that you gather in August
between the roots of alder,
her skin with an odor of wildflowers.

We understand each other perfectly.
We are cousins twice removed.
In the garden we drink our tea,
discussing the plays of Chekhov
as evening falls and the lights begin to twinkle.

But this is only a dream.
I am not there
with my citified speech,
and the old woman is not there
peering between the curtains.

We are only phantoms, bits of ash,
like yesterday's newspaper
or the smoke of chimneys.
All that passed long ago
on a summer night in Odessa.

This is Avram the cello-mender,
the only Jewish sergeant
in the army of the Tsar.
One day he was mending cellos
when they shouted, 'The Tsar is coming,
everyone out for inspection!'
When the Tsar saw Avram marching
with Russians who were seven feet tall,
he said, 'He must be a genius.
I want that fellow at headquarters.'

Luck is given by God.
A wife you must find for yourself.

So Avram married a rich widow
who lived in a house in Odessa.
The place was filled with music . . .
Yasnaya Polyana with noodles.

One night in the middle of a concert
they heard a knock at the door.
So Avram went. It was a beggar,
a Russian, who had been blessed
by God—that is, he was crazy.
And he said, 'I'm a natural son
of the Grand Duke Nicholas.'

And Avram said, 'Eat.
I owe your people a favor.'
And he said, 'My wife is complaining
we need someone to open the door.'
So Nicholas stayed with them for years.
Who ever heard of Jewish people
with a footman?

And then the Germans came. Imagine
the scene—the old people
holding on to their baggage,
and the children—they've been told it's a game,
but they don't believe it.
Then the German says, 'Who's this?'
pointing at Nicholas,
'he doesn't look like a Jew.'
And he said, 'I'm the natural son
of the Grand Duke Nicholas.'
And they saw he was feeble-minded,
and took him away too, to the death-chamber.

'He could have kept his mouth shut',
said my Grandmother,
'but what can you expect.
All of those Romanovs were a little bit crazy.'

In Russia there were three students,
Chaim, Baruch, and Meyer.
'As Maimonides says', said Meyer.
'Speaking of the Flood', said Baruch.
'*Etsev*', said Chaim, 'an equivocal term. . . .'

In Spring when the birch trees shine like crystal
and the light is so clear that a butterfly
makes dark strokes in the air,
there came three students of Hebrew
and the girls from the button-factory—

Dvoira, Malka, Rifkele . . .
a mystery, a fragrance,
and a torment to the scholars.
They couldn't have kept a goat, for the milk,
much less the fastidious girls of our province.

*

One night, the red star rising,
a beautiful dream came to Meyer,
a *moujik* who gave him a kiss,
and he heard a voice say, 'Meyer,
and Lermontov, and Pushkin.'

Dark roofs of Volhynia,
do you remember Meyer
who went to the University
and later he joined the Communist Party?
Last night I dreamed of Meyer. . . .

He turned his head and smiled.
With his hand he made a sign . . .
then his features changed, he was mournful,
and I heard him say in a clear voice,
'Beware! These men killed Meyer.'

THE COUNTRY HOUSE

You always know what to expect
in a novel by L. V. Kalinin. . . .

'One morning in June, in the provincial town
of X, had you been observant,
you might have seen a stranger
alighting at the railroad station.'

From there it moves to a country house,
introduction of the principal characters—
a beautiful girl, a youth
on fire with radical ideas.

There are drawing-room discussions,
picnics at the lake, or a mountain,
if there is one in the vicinity.

Then some misunderstanding—
the young man banished from the house
by the angry father. Tears.

All this with the most meticulous attention
to the 'spirit of the times',
bearing in mind the classical saying,
'Don't be the first to try anything, or the last.'

*

The tone of his letters was quite different:

'The Polish girl I told you about, who is living with us,
has a wart. Two days ago, the idiot
tried to remove it with lye.
For hours on end the house has been filled with howling,
and I can't think or write.'

A NIGHT IN ODESSA

Grandfather puts down his tea-glass
and makes his excuses
and sets off, taking his umbrella.
The street-lamps shine through a fog
and drunkards reel on the pavement.

One man clenches his fists in anger,
another utters terrible sobs. . . .
And women look on calmly.
They like those passionate sounds.
He walks on, grasping his umbrella.

His path lies near the forest.
Suddenly a wolf leaps in the path,
jaws dripping. The man strikes
with the point of his umbrella. . . .
A howl, and the wolf has vanished.

Go on, grandfather, hop!
It takes brains to live here,
not to be beaten and torn
or to lie drunk in a ditch.
Hold on to your umbrella!

He's home. When he opens the door
his wife jumps up to greet him.
Her name is Ninotchka,
she is young and dark and slender,
married only a month or so.

She hurries to get his supper.
But when she puts down the dish
she presses a hand to her side
and he sees that from her hand
red drops of blood are falling.

ISIDOR

Isidor was always plotting
to overthrow the government.
The family lived in one room. . . .
A window rattles,
a woman coughs,
snow drifts over the rooftops . . .
despair. An intelligent household.

One day, there's a knock at the door. . . .
The police! A confusion. . . .
Isidor's wife throws herself
on the mattress . . . she groans
as though she is in labor.
The police search everywhere,
and leave. Then a leg comes out . . .
an arm . . . then a head with spectacles.
Isidor was under the mattress!

When I think about my family
I have a feeling of suffocation.
Next time . . . how about the oven?

The mourners are sitting around
weeping and tearing their clothes.
The inspector comes. He looks in the oven . . .
there's Isidor, with his eyes
shut fast . . . his hands are folded.
The inspector nods, and goes.
Then a leg comes out, and the other.
Isidor leaps, he dances . . .

'Praise God, may His Name be exalted!'

Memory rising in the steppes
flows down. On the banks are trees
and towns with golden cupolas.

I can see my mother's family
sitting around the kitchen stove
arguing—the famous Russian theater.

The sisters return—they're breathless,
they've been down to the river—
their arms filled with wildflowers.

2

Every Friday I used to go to Brooklyn.
Behold the children of Israel
at the end of the Diaspora!

Old men with beards and *yarmelkehs,*
old women sitting on the benches . . .
Israel, is it you?

Talking about their lives in the Old Country. . . .
The passing headlights hurl
their shadows against the wall.

3

Though I walk with a head full of ancient life
it's not that life I see, but houses,
streets, bridges, traffic, crowds, a continual

outpouring of phenomena—
the traffic moving along Broadway,
red glow of the theater district.

I feel I am part of a race
that has not yet arrived in America.
Yet, these people—their faces are strangely familiar.

4

The first clear star comes gliding
over the trees and dark rooftops,
the same world passing here—

voices and shadows of desire,
and the tears of things. . . . Around us
things want to be understood.

And the moon, so softly gleaming
in furs,
that put a hole through Pushkin.

II

Indian Country

INDIAN COUNTRY

1. *The Shadow-hunter*

This prairie light ... I see
a warrior and a child.

The man points, and the child
runs after a butterfly.

Rising and floating in the windy field,
that's how they learned to run ...

Plenty Coups,
Red Cloud, Coyote, Pine Marten.

Now I will lie down in the grass
that Plenty Coups loved.

There are voices in the wind, strong voices
in the tenderness of these leaves,

and the deer move with the shade
into the hills I dream of.

There the young men live by hunting
the shadows of ideas,

and at night they march no further.
Their tents shine in the moonlight.

2. *Black Kettle Raises the Stars and Stripes*

'Nits make lice', said Chivington.
'Kill the nits and you'll get no lice.'

The white men burst in at sunrise, shooting and stabbing.
And there was old Black Kettle
tying the Stars and Stripes to his tent pole,

and the squaws running in every direction

around Sand Creek,
a swept corner of the American consciousness.

And it's no use playing the tuba to a dead Indian.

3. *On the Prairie*

The wind in the leaves makes a sound
like clear running water.

I can smell the store where harness used to be sold. . . .
Morning of little leaves,

morning of cool, clear sunlight,
when the house stirred with the earnestness

of the life they really had . . .
morning with a clang of machinery.

Now an old man sits on the porch;
I can hear it every time he clears his throat . . .

as I stand here, holding the jack,
in the middle of my generation,

by the Lethe of asphalt and dust
and human blood spilled carelessly.

When I look back I see
a field full of grasshoppers.

The hills are hidden with a cloud.
And what pale king sits in the glass?

BALLAD OF ANOTHER OPHELIA

There's an Indian song, an air
called 'Snowflake, you have made me grieve'.

I can hear it still in the stream
falling through the Sierras in August.

She lies in a pine-tree breathing,
or glides on the edge where the stream

pours over, and a branch
jerks up and down in the furious stream.

THE CLIMATE OF PARADISE

A story about Indians,
the tribe that claimed Mt. Shasta. . . .

Five lawyers said, 'It's ridiculous!
What possible use can they have for the mountain?'

The interpreter said, 'Your Honor,
they say that their gods live there.'

*

How different this is from the Buzzy Schofields,
people I met in Pasadena.

Green lawns, imposing villas—
actually, these are caves inhabited

by Pufendorf's dwarfs and Vico's
Big Feet, the 'abandoned by God'.

Thought, says Vico, begins in caves—
but not the Buzzy Schofields'.

They're haunted by Red China—
bugles—a sky lit with artillery.

They're terrified they'll be brainwashed.
They can see themselves breaking under torture . . .

'Stop! I'm on your side!
You're making a terrible mistake!'

O even in Paradise
the mind would make its own winter.

ON THE EVE

There is something sad about property
where it ends, in California.

A patch of white moving in a crack of the fence. . . .
It is the rich widow—
when the dogs howl, she howls like a dog.

*

At night in San Francisco
the businessmen and drunkards
sink down to the ocean floor.

Their lives are passing.
There is nothing in those depths
but the teeth of sharks and the earbones of whales.

Their lives are passing
slowly under the scrutiny
of goggle eyes, in waves that are vaguely

connected to women.
The women stand up in cages
and do it, their breasts in yellow light.

The businessmen of San Francisco
are mildly exhilarated.
Lifting their heavy arms and feet

they stamp on the ocean floor.
They rise from the ooze of the ocean floor
to the lights that float on the surface.

*

It is like night in St. Petersburg.
From the Bay a foghorn sounds,

and ships, wrapped in a mist,
creep out with their heavy secrets
to the war 'that no one wants'.

THE WALL TEST

When they say 'To the wall!'
and the squad does a right turn,

where do you stand? With the squad
or the man against the wall?

In every case
you find yourself standing against the wall.

AMERICAN DREAMS

In dreams my life came toward me,
my loves that were slender as gazelles.
But America also dreams. . . .
Dream, you are flying over Russia,
dream, you are falling in Asia.

As I look down the street
on a typical sunny day in California
it is my house that is burning
and my dear ones that lie in the gutter
as the American army enters.

Every day I wake far away
from my life, in a foreign country.
These people are speaking a strange language.
It is strange to me
and strange, I think, even to themselves.

DOUBTING

I remember the day I arrived.
In the dawn the land seemed clear
and green and mysterious.

I could see the children of Adam
walking among the haystacks;
then, over the bay, a million sparkling windows.

Make room, let me see too!
Let me see how the counters are served
and move with the crowd's excitement the way it goes.

*

Since then so much has changed;
as though Washington, Jefferson, Lincoln
were only money and we didn't have it.

As though the terrible saying of Toqueville
were true: 'There is nothing so sordid . . .
as the life of a man in the States.'

I would like to destroy myself, or failing that,
    my neighbors;
to run in the streets, shouting 'To the wall!'
I would like to kill a hundred, two hundred, a thousand.

I would like to march, to conquer foreign capitals.

*

And there's no end, it seems, to the wars of democracy.
What would Washington, what would Jefferson say
of the troops so heavily armed?

They would think they were Hessians,
and ride back into the hills
to find the people that they knew.

*

I remember another saying:
'It is not the earth, it is not America who is so great . . .'
but 'to form individuals.'

Every day the soul arrives,
and the light on the mental shore
is still as clear, and still it is mysterious.

I can see each tree distinctly.
I could almost reach out
and touch each house, and the hill blossoming with lilacs.

*

I myself am the union of these states,
offering liberty and equality to all.
I share the land equally, I support the arts,

I am developing backward areas.
I look on the negro as myself, I accuse myself
of sociopathic tendencies, I accuse my accusers.

I write encyclopedias and I revise the encyclopedias.
Inside myself there is a record-breaking shot-putter and a
    track team in training.

I send up rockets to the stars.

*

Then once more, suddenly, I'm depressed.
Seeming conscious, falling back,
I sway with the soul's convulsion the way it goes;

and learn to be patient with the soul,
breathe in, breathe out,
and to sit by the bed and watch.

III

Individuals

THE PIHIS

Since first I read in *Zone*
what Apollinaire says of the pihis,
'They have one wing only and fly in a couple'—

I have heard their cries at midnight
and seen the shadows of those passionate
generations of the moon.

PERMISSION TO OPERATE
A MOTOR VEHICLE

The grounds are well laid out
with trees and walks between the buildings,
and the people you meet in the walks
seem positively harmless.

Though many talk to themselves:
'Whaddya mean, fifteen dollars?
Say, lissen, I been aroun!'

I went to Administration, and waited . . .
Time, *Life*, and the *Reader's Digest*.
Then a guide came along, jingling a key-ring,
and took me up to the doctor.
He consulted his files, and talked about the weather,
then wrote in a cheerful scrawl,
'I see no reason why Alexander Philips
should not be permitted
to operate a motor vehicle.
                    L. Mandelbaum, M.D.'

                    *

These have not been permitted:

the grocery-boy, Charlie Hernandez . . .
who struck a guard, who knocked him down,
then the other guard came running,
and they kicked with the points of their shoes
in the ribs and the belly,
and so, a day later, Charlie Hernandez died.

And the man who makes a whistling sound
and 'Bang!' Then he says in a loud voice,
'This is it. Fix bayonets!'

And the man who comes toward me
with a newspaper, whispering . . .
something to do with a woman.

And the case of the crying girl.

'So you made it', they say, and
'Yes', I say, then we are silent,

listening to the noises of the street . . .
a distant sound of traffic,
footsteps, the restaurant awnings
that flap in the wind.

THE PHOTOGRAPHER

A bearded man seated on a camp-stool—
'The geologist. 1910.'

'Staying with friends'—a boy in a straw hat,
on a porch, surrounded with wisteria.

'Noontime'—a view of the Battery
with masts passing over the rooftops.

Then the old horse-cars on Broadway,
people standing around in the garment district.

A high view of Manhattan,
light-shelves with sweeps of shadow.

'Jumpers'—as they come plunging down
their hair bursts into fire.

Then there are photographs of a door-knob,
a chair, an unstrung tennis-racket.

'Still life. Yes, for a while.
It gives your ideas a connection.

And a beautiful woman yawning
with the back of her hand, like this.'

SIMPLICITY

Climbing the staircase
step by step, feeling my way . . .
I seem to have some trouble with my vision.
The stairs are littered with paper,
eggshells, and other garbage.
Then she comes to the door.
Without eye-shadow or lipstick,
with her hair tied in a bun,
in a white dress, she seems ethereal.

'Peter', she says, 'how nice!
I thought that you were Albert,
but he hardly ever comes.'

She says, 'I hope you like my dress.
It's simple. I made it myself.
Nowadays everyone's wearing simple things.
The thing is to be sincere,
and then, when you're tired of something,
you just throw it away.'

I'll spare you the description
of all her simple objects:
the bed pushed in one corner;
the naked bulb that hangs
on a wire down from the ceiling
that is stamped out of metal
in squares, each square containing
a pattern of leaves and flowers;
the window with no blinds, admitting
daylight, and the wall
where a stream of yellow ice hangs down
in waves.

      She is saying
'I have sat in this room

all day. There is a time
when you just stare at the wall
all day, and nothing moves.
I can't go on like this any longer,
counting the cracks in the wall,
doting on my buttons.'

I seem to be disconnected
from the voice that is speaking
and the sound of the voice that answers.
Things seem to be moving into a vacuum.
I put my head in my hands
and try to concentrate.
But the light shines through my hands,

and then (how shall I put it
exactly?) it's as though she begins
giving off vibrations,
waves of resentment, an aura
of hate you could cut with a knife. . . .
Squirming, looking over her shoulder. . . .
Her whole body seems
to shrink, and she speaks in hisses:

'They want to remove my personality.
They're giving me psychotherapy
and *ikebana*, the art of flower-arrangement.
Some day, I suppose, I'll be cured,
and then I'll go and live in the suburbs,
doting on dogs and small children.'

I go down the stairs, feeling my way
step by step. When I come out,
the light on the snow is blinding.
My shoes crunch on ice and my head
goes floating along, and a voice
from a high, barred window cries
'Write me a poem!'

VANDERGAST AND THE GIRL

Vandergast to his neighbors—
the grinding of a garage door
and hiss of gravel in the driveway.

He worked for the insurance company
whose talisman is a phoenix
rising in flames . . . *non omnis moriar*.
From his desk he had a view of the street—

translucent raincoats, and umbrellas,
fluorescent plate-glass windows.
A girl knelt down, arranging
underwear on a female dummy—

sea waves and, on the gale,
Venus, these busy days,
poised in her garter-belt and stockings.

                    *

The next day he saw her eating
in the restaurant where he usually ate.

Soon they were having lunch together
elsewhere.

                She came from Dallas.
This was only a start, she was ambitious,
twenty-five and still unmarried.
Green eyes with silver spiricles . . .
red hair. . . .

                When he held the car door open
her legs were smooth and slender.

'I was wondering',
she said, 'when you'd get round to it',
and laughed.

     *

Vandergast says he never intended
having an affair.

     And was that what this was?
The names that people give to things. . . .
What do definitions and divorce-court proceedings
have to do with the breathless reality?

O little lamp at the bedside
with views of Venice and the Bay of Naples,
you understood! *Lactona* toothbrush
and suitcase bought in a hurry,
you were the witnesses of the love
we made in bed together.

Schrafft's Chocolate Cherries, surely you remember
when she said she'd be true forever,

and, watching 'Dark Storm', we decided
there is something to be said, after all,
for soap opera, 'if it makes people happy.'

     *

The Vandergasts are having some trouble
finding a buyer for their house.

When I go for a walk with Tippy
I pass the unweeded tennis court,
the empty garage, windows heavily shuttered.

Mrs. Vandergast took the children
and went back to her family.

And Vandergast moved to New Jersey,
where he works for an insurance company
whose emblem is the Rock of Gibraltar—
the rest of his life laid out
with the child-support and alimony payments.

As for the girl, she vanished.

Was it worth it? Ask Vandergast.
You'd have to be Vandergast, looking through his eyes
at the house across the street, in Orange, New Jersey.
Maybe on wet days umbrellas and raincoats
set his heart thudding.

                Maybe
he talks to his pillow, and it whispers,
moving red hair.

In any case, he will soon be forty.

Her face turned sour.
It broke into tears.
She wept, she wept.
The streams were wide and deep.
Wide and deep were the streams
of time that were flowing toward me.
Neither she nor I could control
the flow of her tears,
and so, in the middle of summer,
this tender girl and I
were married in rain-water.

CYNTHIA

There are ghosts after all

'But his family all wore black,
and besides, Cynthia doesn't speak Belgian,
so she returned to America
and had an abortion,
and the doctor, the abortionist. . . .'

Go on. Continue.

'After an abortion, you know, there's a fear
of anything coming in.
Now she lives in fear of the Mafia
and keeps her door on the chain.'

Itzel who comes on like an octopus
with the Bhagavad-gita,
and the sayings of Lao-tze,
Gandhi, and Blake, and Jesus.

Om mane podne ohm.

Itzel with his beads and black-rimmed spectacles
standing outside the municipal building
with the outraged citizens shouting
'Go back where you came from!'
And, 'This is a Christian community.'

One Itzel, two Itzels, three . . .
beads, beards, bells, sandals, and Indian feathers.
'Throw them to the lions!'

Om.

ON A DISAPPEARANCE
OF THE MOON

And I, who used to lie with the moon,
am here in a peat-bog.

With a criminal, an adulterous girl,
and a witch tied down with branches . . .

the glaucous eyeballs gleaming
under the lids, some hairs still on the chin.

AN AMERICAN PEASANT

I am swept in a taxi
to the door of a friend.
He greets me like a statue
fixed in the position of a man
who always marries the wrong woman.

Then he starts to argue—about Black Power,
Che Guevara, the SDS.
He is hardening into an attitude
and becoming an authority.
He is writing a series of political articles.

There are little bits of toilet-paper
where he's cut himself shaving.

Through a window I can see the park
with people sitting on the benches.
The Fifth Avenue bus goes by,
then a man with a white cane . . .

then a dog, crossing the road at an angle.
It must have discovered something
mixed with the odor of crank-case oil
and dust, a delirious
fragrance of sexual life.

'What's the use . . . you're not listening!'

You're right. I have always lived
as though I knew the reason.
Like a peasant I trust in silence.
And I don't believe in ideas
unless they are unavoidable.

Only yesterday, Thanksgiving,
in the middle of dinner
as I rocked to and fro with a toothache,
my wife said, 'At last
you have learned *dahvinen* . . . to pray.'

IV

Looking for Chekhov's House

PORT JEFFERSON

My whole life coming to this place,
and understanding it better
maybe for having been born
offshore, and at an early age
left to my own support . . .

I have come where sea and wind,
wave and leaf, are one sighing,
where the house strains at an anchor
and the salt-rose clings and clambers
on the humorous grave.

This is the place, Camerado,
that hides the sea-bird's nest.
Listening to the distant voices
in summer, a murmur of the sea,
I seem to remember everything.

Look through the telescope
see she said

I looked it looked
like a shilling

We'll go in the moon
Daddy said

In the twenties
a Moon was a big touring car

2

white sand
blue waves
nobody ever
misbehaves

it's nice to live in a British colony
says the Duchess of
Cumuppingshire

O to be a
nightingale
now that Endland's
here

O I don't know
says the Duke
I think it's a lot of belly rot

blue sand
white waves
jolly good chaps
in nigger graves

3

The natives are dancing
Maud come into the garden
and see the people dancing

See, that one's a
rooster
and that one's

a horse
It's called John Canoe
Peculiar   Of course

Driven by the wind, black billows
surge, and the sand is littered.
Deep, deep in the interior
the temple of the god is hidden.

On slopes overgrown with vines
and thorns, where bees are humming,
with wide, complacent eyes
the wooden face stares calmly.

THE LAST OF IT

Why are you walking the lane
that leads down to the house
where a still light is shining?

In the house there is a room
where a man stares at the wall
all day and does not move.

A woman stands by the light
watching the sick man breathe.
Her hair is the redness of gold.

But that was long ago.
Your father has gone from the house,
the woman is withered and old.

Life, the interesting character
tugging at my mind, 'Hey mister!',

is weird: El Fusilado,
who 'received 8 bullets

through the body and head
and the *coup de grâce*, yet LIVED!';

deep: a subway-grating fisher,
letting his line down through the sidewalk,

in the shadows of the rocks
and the tall pines leaning over;

romantic: an old red-headed woman,
sixty if she's a day,

taking her stand outside the theatre
that features 'Naked Sin'.

A FRIEND OF THE FAMILY

Once upon a time in California
the ignorant married the inane
and they lived happily ever after.

But nowadays in the villas
with swimming-pools shaped like a kidney
technicians are beating their wives.
They're accusing each other of mental cruelty.

And the children of those parents
are longing for a rustic community.
They want to get back to the good old days.

Coming toward me . . . a slender
sad girl dressed like a sailor . . .
she says, 'Do you have any change?'

One morning when the Mother Superior
was opening another can of furniture polish
Cyd ran for the bus
and came to San Francisco.
Now she drifts from pad to pad. 'Hey mister',
she says, 'do you have any change?
I mean, for a hamburger. Really.'

2

Let Yevtushenko celebrate the construction
of a hydroelectric dam.
For Russians a dam that works is a miracle.

Why should we celebrate it?
There are lights in the mountain states,
sanatoriums, and the music of Beethoven.

Why should we celebrate the construction
of a better bowling-alley?
Let Yevtushenko celebrate it.

A hundred, that's how ancient it is
with us, the rapture of material conquest,
democracy 'draining a swamp,
turning the course of a river'.

The dynamo howls
but the psyche is still, like an Indian.

And those who are still distending the empire
have vanished beyond our sight.
Far from the sense of hearing
and touch, they are merging
with Asia . . .

expanding the war on nature
and the old know-how to Asia.

Nowadays if we want that kind of excitement—
selling beads and whiskey to Indians,
setting up a feed-store,
a market in shoes, tires, machineguns,
material ecstasy, money with hands and feet
stacked up like wooden Indians . . .

we must go out to Asia,
or rocketing outward in space.

3

What are they doing in Russia
these nights for entertainment?

In our desert where gaspumps shine
the women are changing their hair—
bubbles of gold and magenta . . .

and the young men yearning to be off
full speed . . . like Chichikov

in a troika-rocket, plying
the whip, while stars go flying
(Too bad for the off-beat horse!)

These nights when a space-rocket rises
and everyone sighs 'That's Progress!'
I say to myself 'That's Chichikov.'

As it is right here on earth—
osteopaths on Mars,
actuaries at the Venus-Hilton . . .
Chichikov talking, Chichikov eating,
Chichikov making love.

'Hey Chichikov, where are you going?'

'I'm off to the moon', says Chichikov.

'What will you do when you get there?'

'How do I know?' says Chichikov.

4

Andrei, that fish you caught was my uncle.
He lived in Lutsk, not to be confused
with Lodz which is more famous.

When he was twenty he wrote to Chekhov,
and an answer came—'Come to us.'
And there it was, signed 'Chekhov'.

I can see him getting on the train.
It was going to the great city
where Jews had been forbidden.

He went directly to Chekhov's house.
At the door he saw a crowd . . .
they told him that Chekhov had just died.

So he went back to his village.
Years passed . . . he danced at a wedding
and wept at a funeral. . . .

Then, when Hitler sent for the Jews
he said, 'And don't forget Isidor . . .
turn left at the pickle-factory.'

Andrei, all my life I've been haunted
by Russia—a plain,
a cold wind from the *shtetl*.

I can hear the wheels of the train.
It is going to Radom,
it is going to Jerusalem. . . .

In the night where candles shine
I have a luminous family . . .
people with their arms round each other

forever.

5

I can see myself getting off the train.
'Say, can you tell me how to get. . . .'

To Chekhov's house perhaps?

That's what everyone wants, and yet
Chekhov was just a man . . . with ideas,
it's true. As I said to him once,
Where on earth do you meet those people?

Vanya who is long-suffering
and Ivanov who is drunk.

And the man, I forget his name,
who thinks everything is forbidden . . .
that you have to have permission
to run, to shout. . . .

And the people who say, 'Tell us,
what is it you do exactly to justify your existence?'

These idiots rule the world,
Chekhov knew it, and yet
I think he was happy, on his street.
People live here . . . you'd be amazed.

V

The Foggy Lane

THE FOGGY LANE

The houses seem to be floating
in the fog, like lights at sea.

Last summer I came here with a man
who spoke of the ancient Scottish poets—
how they would lie blindfolded,
with a stone placed on the belly,
and so compose their panegyrics . . .
while we, being comfortable, find nothing to praise.

Then I came here with a radical
who said that everything is corrupt;
he wanted to live in a pure world.

And a man from an insurance company
who said that I needed 'more protection'.

Walking in the foggy lane
I try to keep my attention fixed
on the uneven, muddy surface . . .
the pools made by the rain,
and wheel-ruts, and wet leaves,
and the rustling of small animals.

I am taking part in a great experiment—
whether writers can live peacefully in the suburbs
and not be bored to death.

As Whitman said, an American muse
installed amid the kitchen ware.
And we have wonderful household appliances . . .
now tell me about the poets.

Where are your children, Lucina?
Since Eliot died and Pound
has become . . . an authority,
chef d'école au lieu d'être tout de go,

I have been listening to the whispers
of U.S. Steel and Anaconda:
'In a little while it will stiffen . . .
blown into the road,

drifting with the foam of chemicals.'

2

The light that shines through the *Leaves*
is clear: 'to form individuals.'

A swamp where the seabirds brood.
When the psyche is still and the soul does nothing,
a Sound, with shining tidal pools and channels.

And the kingdom is within you . . .
the hills and all the streams
running west to theMississippi.
There the roads are lined with timothy
and the clouds are tangled with the haystacks.

Your loves are a line of birch trees.
When the wind flattens the grass, it
shines, and a butterfly
writes dark lines on the air.

There are your sacred objects,
the wings and gazing eyes
of the life you really have.

                    3
Where then shall we meet?

                              Where you left me.

At the drive-in restaurant . . .
the fields on either side covered with stubble,
an odor of gasoline and burning asphalt,
glare on tinted glass, chrome-plated hubcaps and bumpers.

I came out, wiping my hands
on my apron, to take your orders.
Thin hands, streaked with mustard,
give us a hot-dog,
give us a Pepsi-Cola.

Listening to the monotonous grasshoppers
for years I have concentrated on the moment.

And at night when the passing headlights hurl
shadows flitting across the wall,
I sit in a window, combing my hair
day in day out.

On days like this I rush to the pencil-sharpener.
The hours pass unnoticed.
On a writing-table, in chairs
and corners, in folds of a sunlit curtain,
the touch of a woman lingers.

YEN YU

Talking about the *avant-garde* in China
long ago in the 13th century—

'The worst of them', said Yen Yu,
'even scream and growl,
and besides, they use abusive language.
Poetry like this is a disaster.'

He said, 'Do you see this ant?
Observe, when he meets a procession,
how he pauses, putting out feelers,
and then turns back, in the "new direction".
That way he stays out front.'

And he said, 'Avoid bad poets,
even if they are in the *avant-garde*.'

My girl the voluptuous creature
was shaving her legs and saying, 'Darling,
if poetry comes not as naturally
as the leaves to a tree
it had better not come at all.'

'Och', I said, 'and the sorra
be takin your English Johnny!
What, is a poet a thing without brains in its head?
If wishing could do it, I'd compose
poems as grand as physics,
poems founded in botany, psychology, biology,
poems as progressive as the effect
of radiation on a foetus.'

She turned on the switch of her razor
and said, 'When you talk about poetry
it reminds me of a man in long underwear
doing barbell exercises.
His biceps bulge. In the meantime
outside on the gaslit street
his wife, a voluptuous lady,
elopes with a "swell" who takes her
to Lindy's for oysters,
from there to the Waldorf, and there
on a bed carved like seashells
they move, while the man with the barbells
by gaslight is marching
and swinging his arms to the tune of the *Washington Post*.'

I went to the window. It was night,
and the beautiful moon
was stealing away to meet someone.
The bitches! They want to feel wanted,
and everything else is prose.

TRASIMENO

When Hannibal defeated the Roman army
he stopped at Trasimeno.

That day, and the next, he marched no further.
His tent lay in the moonlight,

his sword shone in the moonlight,
what thought kept him from moving, no one knows.

Stranger, when you go to Rome,
when you have placed your hand in the gargoyle's mouth,

and walked in the alleys . . .
when you have satisfied your hunger for stone,

at night you will return to the trees
and the ways of the barbarians,

hands, eyes, voices, ephemera,
shadows of the African horsemen.

He was one of the consorts of the moon,
and went with the goddess in a cart.

Wherever he went there would be someone,
a few of the last of the old religion.

Here the moon passes behind a cloud.
Fifteen centuries pass,

then one of the bog-peat cutters
digs up the man—with the rope

that ends in a noose at the throat—
a head squashed like a pumpkin.

Yet, there is delicacy in the features
and a peaceful expression . . .

that in Spring the flower comes forth
with a music of pipes and dancing.

THE SILENT PIANO

We have lived like civilized people.
O ruins, traditions!

And we have seen the barbarians,
breakers of sculpture and glass.

And now we talk of 'the inner life',
and I ask myself, where is it?

Not here, in these streets and houses,
so I think it must be found

in indolence, pure indolence,
an ocean of darkness,

in silence, an arm of the moon,
a hand that enters slowly.

*

I am reminded of a story
Camus tells, of a man in prison camp.

He had carved a piano keyboard
with a nail on a piece of wood.

And sat there playing the piano.
This music was made entirely of silence.